Introductic

These devotional songs and dances grew out of many years of fa
seekers. Music, voice and movement were integral to those sessi
nourish spiritual awakening and worship. I wanted to use more th
limited supply. Perhaps centuries of puritanical influence had suc
some degree in so many parts of the Christian tradition.

However, there has been a huge revival of interest in recent years. Many individuals and organisations, such as the Taizé and Iona Communities, have been leading the way in developing new works and reviving old ones. All the songs on this CD are new, as are some of the dances (the others being developed from other well known ones). They arose in part from a desire to develop pieces in my own language and which speak to that mystical and contemplative approach to the Divine - the longing for union and the challenges that longing raises. All the words used are rooted in the Christian tradition, but I know they have been sung, heard and developed by people from other traditions and none. That is my intention; that they be available to all regardless of the particular Way Home you have chosen.

Some of the phrases may be challenging to those who are not from a Christian background (and to some who are!) but I have offered short explanations before each one to illuminate the meaning and purpose. They also accompany the main themes in my recent book "Coming Home – notes for the journey", which provides much more detailed exploration of the spiritual principles and practices underpinning each song and dance. I make no claims to be theologically sound, for these songs and dances are not about theology, but about the heartfelt search for a relationship to the Divine that is personal and immanent. They seek to express something of the soul's desire to be free of the limitations of the ego's demands, to transform our way of being in the world.

The songs all arose whilst visiting some of my favourite places of spiritual renewal - invariably outdoors in the wildness of the elements; the island and abbey of Iona, the friary and long beach at Alnmouth, the mountains of my home in Cumbria. In fact the first song written down ("Ego sum") came to me whilst sitting on top of Dun-I on Iona, remembering my mother and being cradled and rocked when I was ill as a child. There are such remembrances in all of these songs, may you find yours too. With one exception (song 17) all the words are taken from the Old and New Testaments simply because they have inspired me. They are not used to proselytise, but to encourage and illuminate, to be enjoyed alone or in companionship and connection with others. They offer insights and meanings that may be otherwise overlooked just by reading. They seek to nourish through words, music and movement a deepening connection with God, for each is also a prayer of body, heart, mind and soul - an act of devotion before the Divine.

The sequence is not random, for each of these 19 works is part of a narrative, touching upon the soul's desire to break free and return Home. They can be followed in the order set out in these pages or dipped into at random as preferred. The arrangements provide a basic set of harmonies and rhythms, but feel free to adjust these and develop them as you wish. For example, when I first introduced "I am the Way" to a group, they very quickly not only got into the rhythm of it, but spontaneously broke out into harmonies, multiple shades of volume and so forth. Another time a group took the "Ego Sum" chant and slowed it down to a soft gentle rhythm, adding more harmonies and instruments and repeating it so that it lasted for over 30 minutes. Others have told me that they find listening to some of the chants in solitude helpful for meditation or enjoyed by simply singing them repetitively whilst doing other things.

May these words, music and dances bring blessings into your life and draw you a little closer to the One from whom you came.

Stephen G Wright
Mungrisdale
2010

Lord, save me

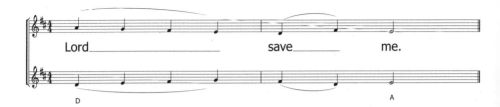

Lord_____ save_____ me.

D   A

1. "Lord, save me"

For many people the spiritual quest, the search for the Way Home, begins (or is given a push!) in moments that are challenging, when our old ways of doing things seem to come unstuck, when our customary values and perceptions are thrown into disarray. It can be extreme, feeling like we are drowning, under attack, overwhelmed and unable to cope as the storms of life batter us. We may feel disconnected from the Divine, abandoned, helpless, like we are "going under", alone – this can be a terrifying place to be, hell. In the New Testament (Matthew 14:30) one of the shortest of all prayers for just such a moment is made clear. To the astonishment of the disciples, Jesus walks across the sea to them amidst a storm. The disciple Peter attempts to walk on the water too, but he becomes distracted and frightened. His attention gone from Jesus, he soon sinks and is about to drown. He gasps "Lord, save me!" Jesus reaches down and takes his hand. The story is rich with symbolism. It exemplifies our limitations, our need to surrender and ask for help, in humility, to be open to the faith that there is One available to us willing to help. As we set out on the Way Home, we long to be free of suffering and the relentless drowning demands and desires of the ego, of everyday personhood and identity. A heartfelt prayer for help arises in us - "Lord, save me!"

The Dance reflects this sense of being isolated yet aware that help is in reach even though we may be full of doubt. We stand alone recognising the essential (at least superficially) separateness of human beings and our aloneness in the face of what is besetting us. And yet, prayerfully aware and in expectation, we sense and hope that we are not alone; help is at hand.

Stand in a circle, join hands (V hold – that is holding hands hanging by side) then spread the circle a little to ensure enough space for each. Let go of hands and place your own hands together on your heart. Stand with feet a little apart; eyes downcast. Sway gently (first to the right) to the rhythm of the chant from side to side (four beats each way). Continue.

Ego sum

2. "Ego sum, noli timere"

In the same story from Matthew (14:22-33) the disciples' terror of the storm is matched only by their fear at the sight of Jesus walking over the sea to them. "Do not be afraid, it is I", He says (in Latin "Ego sum, noli timere" – I first heard it expressed this way in school long ago). Thus, in crying out for help, the prospect of God approaching us in response may itself be terrifying. And is Jesus also saying that the storm is "I" too? That somehow the Divine is present not just in what we judge pleasant or comfortable, but also in that which we find frightening? That there is nowhere that God is not even in our darkest moments? The chant has a lullaby quality to it, as if we are being held and comforted, rocked like a baby in the arms of one who loves us. Along the Way we experience much joy and bliss, but we also encounter fear and sadness – perhaps making us feel that we must give up. The song offers us comfort, reminds us that we are never alone and invites us to embrace the ever present God; to remember that we are held even though we may doubt it in difficult times.

The Dance encourages supporting one another amidst the movement of the stormy sea, as we advance and open to the centre, to the Source of All; willing to receive what the Divine has to offer us. We are not alone. There is an eternal voice of comfort. No need to fear, we are gathered in the circle with each other and with God.

Stand in a circle, join hands (V hold).
Part 1 - Four steps towards centre, start with right foot, to the beat of "Ego sum, noli timere". Let go of hands while walking in, then place arms behind low back of neighbour on either side. After four steps, stand and sway right and left, right and left.
Part 2 - Four steps backwards (start with right foot), let hands drift away from neighbours' back and return to V hold. Stand and sway right and left, right and left.
Continue.

I have called you by name

3. "I have called you by name"

Many people are introduced to God as a forbidding, remote power always ready to punish us. But a primary Christian message is that God is Love. Furthermore, this love is not just general to all of creation but also specific to each one of us individually and uniquely. In the Old Testament Book of Isaiah (43:1-7) God speaks to the people Israel to remind them that He has called them by name, that they are precious to Him, that He loves them, that they need not be afraid. I have often used this text to explore its rich symbolism with seekers (taken at face value, some of it can be difficult) not least to insert their own name in place of Israel. It can be life changing for some people to realise that they are personally, uniquely, individually loved by God. As we sing this song, we may not only imagine these words being spoken directly to us by God, but also notice the effect when we sing these same words back to God. Thus we explore the love of God and the God of love as close, personal and mutual - available for each one, for each one of us is "precious" and "called by name".

The Dance is also a heart-centred body prayer acknowledging the love of the Divine offered to us personally and generally, and offering it back in return. As God speaks these words to us we open to embrace and accept them, and return them. Love speaks to love.

Stand in a circle, join hands and stand apart. Let go of hands and stand with legs slightly apart, hands resting on solar plexus palms inwards.
Part 1 - With the 1st "I have called you by name" let the knees bend slightly, slowly separate and move the hands down and outwards in front and up to heart level, gathering in again this time bringing the hands to rest over each other on the heart space, while straightening the knees.
Part 2 - With the 2nd "I have called you by name" let the arms stretch out from the heart, knees bending slightly at the same time as before. Let the palms face forward, spreading the arms outwards and upwards and round to over the head height, bringing hands together palms facing outwards, knees straightening while doing so.
Part 3 - As you begin to hear "You are precious to me" at the top of arc, fold the hands down and over each other while at head height, then gradually bring palms (now facing inwards) down to rest over the heart.
Part 4 - As the words "and I love you" are heard sway right, sway left, step right, side close left. Finish with a deep bow bending at the knee and return to upright position whilst slowly replacing hands over solar plexus.
Repeat parts 1 – 4 then at the short interval – side right, close left and take deep bow bending at the knees once more.
Continue from beginning.

The long road

Call and response

The	night	is	dark,	the	road	is	long.
I	feel	the	love	that	draws	me	near,
	Called	to	serve,	I	wait	for	You.
I	give	my -	self	a -	way	in	You.
Sur -	ren -	der	calls	me	deep -	er	in.
	Turn	me,	Lord,	oh	turn	me	round
The	night	is	dark,	the	road	is	long.

Home,   home,   You   call   me   home.

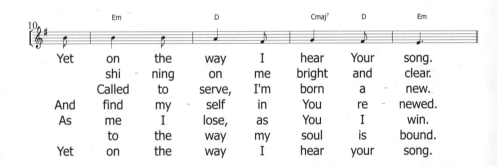

Yet	on	the	way	I	hear	Your	song.
	shi -	ning	on	me	bright	and	clear.
	Called	to	serve,	I'm	born	a -	new.
And	find	my -	self	in	You	re -	newed.
As	me	I	lose,	as	You	I	win.
	to	the	way	my	soul	is	bound.
Yet	on	the	way	I	hear	your	song.

Home,   home,   You   call   me   home.

4. "The long road"

"God gives the desolate a home to live in." (Psalm 68:6). Offered a personal relationship with God, we set out on our Way to deepen that connection, to explore all that it can mean to us. We encounter many struggles as we do so, as well as times of joy and connection. However lost and fearful we may become, whatever distractions and terrors come our way, we seem somehow programmed to respond to that call Home, to hear that voice and keep following it as we shed our fears and doubts. We become less likely to fall back into forgetting especially when the demands of "ordinary" life seem to be in conflict with the promptings of the "spiritual" life. (Along the Way we learn to question that duality.) Somehow we come to know that there is an inexorable magnetic pull at work, like some bell summoning us in the distance, that draws us ever onwards, an insistent voice somewhere that calls us Home and provides a compass point for direction.

The Dance reflects the sense of walking, journeying, along the Way and the challenges that are to be met; whilst always the call Home is there in our lives whether we hear it or not. The call and response of the songs echoes the doubts and difficulties we face, yet also the hopeful message of faith that we are being aided and the call Home never abandons us.

Stand in a circle, (V) hold hands, facing left. Anticlockwise step right, then left, then right, then left. Let go of hands, turn around right shoulder (the turn takes place with each chorus) letting right arm form gentle arc in front palm uppermost, left arm by side. Turn in four steps. Join hands again.
Continue.

I Search

5. "I search"

As we commit to the search, a sense of isolation is a common experience, the feeling that it is all "down to us". We may forget that a helper is always present. When Jesus says "I am with you always" (Matthew 28:20) he does not say – "but only on the good days, or when you are being nice, or providing that..." but *always*. In learning to forge a new relationship of trust with the Divine, we call out for a guiding light. And always, the compassionate God waits, replying in consolation to re-mind us of His presence often when we feel most lost.

The Dance is slow, gentle and purposeful, as we move from person to person to face each other. We acknowledge each other as we search along the Way, then pause and bow. In doing so we remember the Divine is always right here wherever we are, in each of us - mirroring back to us in each person, in the creation, in the Presence.

Partner dance. Form a circle and face partner.
Part 1 - With "I search in the daytime..." dance in a "grand chain" - right palm to right palm to start, then right and left steps to pass first partner, passing partner by right shoulder, proceed to next person, then palm to palm with left hand and step right and left past each other's left shoulder. Continue twice more reaching 5th person to "I call out..."
Part 2 - With 5th person, pause and face each other, both palms to palms. Gradually raise palms overhead together from middle of body, spreading outwards in a wide circle along with "I call out where are you..." until hands are together overhead, only fingers touching with "... comes clear". With "I am here" – gradually separate hands from partner, bring your own hands together in gesture of prayer. Bow a little lower three times with each of the three phrases "I am here" until bowing at the waist.
Continue.

I am the Way

I am the Way, the Truth and the Life.

I am the Way, the Truth and the Life.

Keyboard

Am   Em   Am

I am the Way, the Truth and the Life.

I am the Way, the Truth and the Life

C   Em   Am

6. "I am the Way"

The spiritual search can be full of blind alleys and deceptions along the Way. In an age of the spiritual supermarket, where everything is on offer, it can be hard to discern the deep from the shallow, the true from the false. Books, teachers, gurus, courses – we have these in abundance, and coming to know which is authentic is part of the emergence of spiritual maturity and skilfulness. Jesus, in his great "I am" sayings, offers us insights into the nature of the true spiritual servant-master. The statement "I am the Way" (John 14:6) has been much abused, to justify intolerance and exclusivity, but Jesus offers us far richer possibilities in these words (see for example Neil Douglas-Klotz' excellent discussion in "The Hidden Gospel", Quest Books 1999). In the rich and often mystical language of Aramaic, the language Jesus spoke, he was not only telling us something about himself as a person, but about the very nature of "I am-ness" itself, the unity of the Divine and the creation. He offers us His Way, His life, as a template, an exemplar of how to pray, to relate to others, to live our lives in relation to God. As we awaken to the wonder of the journey Home, of all the possibilities in the limitlessness of God, we need a guide, a teacher, a friend - one who has already trodden the Way and knows its joys and its struggles. Jesus offers a Way, map and compass, but also reminds us that such guidance is not in some far off place or person or just the wise teacher. The "I am" is within – he reminds us of this when he says "You are the light" (Matthew 5:14) and "The Kingdom of God is among you" (Luke 17:21).

The Dance joins everyone together for we are all bound for the same Home. As we advance we bow to honour the Divine, gifting us with guidance along the Way; as we lean back we receive the gifts being offered. In so doing we sing to honour the One who calls us, but also reflect that the Way, the Truth and the Life rest in each one of us, ready to be awakened.

Join hands in a circle. Clockwise movement. Short step left and at the same time soften knees and bow slightly swaying forward to "I am". Slide close right and in doing so let the upper body return to upright and sway back a little to "the Way". Repeat movement, this time moving forwards to "the Truth" and swaying back to "the Life".
Continue.
(If desired, one person can break the circle and lead the group spiralling inwards into tight spiral then back outwards to reform the circle.)

My Heart Longs for You

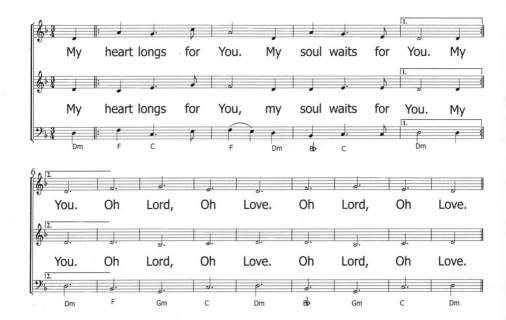

7. "My heart longs"

The longing to find our Way Home powers the spiritual quest. It can feel painful at times, as the journey seems endless, but the longing is also what drives us onward in the search. We thirst to be quenched, hunger to be fed. In Psalm 42:1 this is expressed as a deer longing for flowing streams - "so my soul longs for you".

The Dance reminds us of the search for the Divine only to discover, in humility, that God is in the place where we stand. Notice that the slow rocking backwards and forwards in a gesture of prayer marks the shape of the cross.

Stand in a circle, Join hands, face centre, V hold. Anticlockwise movement.
Part 1 - "My heart longs..." Face centre, side step right, cross left in front, sway right and left (in rhythm quick/quick/slow/slow) x four. Let go of hands and bring up to prayer position.
Part 2 – With "Oh, Lord..." Rock in with right foot, back left. ¼ swivel on left foot to left, again rock out and in, ¼ swivel to left, rock out and in and back, ¼ to left rock out and in. Join hands again quickly.
Continue.

Call me Home

8. "Call me Home"

As the search continues, we come to realise more and more how easy it is to get lost, distracted, forgetting to listen to the One voice that is drawing us along the Way. In these times of disconnection we may also realise how very little power we have to control the whole process on the Way, that indeed it is the Way, through Divine grace, that is pulling us and we need its constant calling to remind us; we need its power, its spirit to break through when we wander.

The Dance reflects the sense of onward motion, whilst also acknowledging that the spiritual journey, in response to the impulse of the Divine is not so much about length but depth, turning in on ourselves to be open to the pull of the Divine while being grounded in our earthly life at the same time.

Stand in a circle, face centre, V hold. Anticlockwise movement.
Part 1 - "Call me Home" - Side step right, cross left in front, side step right, cross left behind. (Grapevine)
Part 2 - "Amen"- Let go of hands, right arm raise palm uppermost, look up to right hand whilst left arm is down with palm facing earth, turn on the spot stepping right, left, right, left. Join hands again.
Continue.

Kyrie

9. "Kyrie"

One of the greatest teachings in our spiritual maturation, arguably the greatest teaching, is that of humility. As we learn that we have little power ourselves, then where will the help come from? If we are beset by difficulties, who is on our side? The words to this dance are the Greek translation of the "Jesus Prayer" – "Kyrie Jesu Christe Eleison" – "Lord Jesus Christ have mercy". I have used the Greek version here in part because I love the sound of the words, but also because of its ancient echoes. This prayer can be difficult for anyone unfamiliar with it, and to modern ears the words can be very loaded (see also Dance 11). The prayer is drawn from the story of blind Bartimaeus in Luke (18:35-43) when he cries out to Jesus to have mercy on him. It was developed further (and became known as the "Jesus Prayer") through the 7th century writings of John Climacus and later embraced as a major spiritual practice in the Russian Orthodox Church. It has seen something of a revival in recent years in Western Christianity. The understanding of "mercy" has tended to be distorted by views of mediaeval knights holding back from killing an opponent, but in fact the word means "compassion". Compassion is more than feeling sorry for someone or having empathy for their plight, it is a willingness to act with love to help another. The blind beggar asks for Jesus' help quite directly. Thus on our spiritual search we learn to ask for help, to turn towards the Source, to acknowledge that we cannot do it all under our own steam, that we need the love of the Divine to save us from our doubts, distractions and disconnections.

The Dance suggests a movement towards the centre, the Source, asking for help, reminding us where the centre lies, before we continue our search.

Stand in a circle, face centre, V hold. Anticlockwise movement.
Part 1 – Quite slow steps with inward movement diagonally right, left, right , left to centre while slowly raising arms to W position at same time, ¼ swivel to left then four steps backwards diagonally starting with right foot and lower arms slowly at same time back to V position. ¼ swivel to the right and repeat from the start.
Part 2 - At the musical interlude in the chant, sway right and left, right and left with hands in V hold.
Continue.
[An alternative is to double the speed of the steps (but not the sways) in part one, increasing to four (from two) the sequence in this part, if you want a "pacier" dance.]

The Light Shines

10. "The light shines"

These words in the opening verses of John's gospel (1:5) are full of hope. Despite the challenges on our Way, we are reassured that there is always light in the darkness, and that it cannot be overcome. Staying with that awareness in prayer and meditation can sustain us as we face the next steps or seek to discover whatever is holding us back.

The Dance has quite a vigorous, joyful rhythm. We know we are being helped by an ever present light along our Way, whether we are always aware of it or not.

Stand in a circle; join hands, V hold. Anticlockwise movement.
Part 1 - With "The light shines..." - forward right then left/right on the spot on toes (i.e. waltz step - long, short, short) then left forward, right/left on the spot on toes. Six times.
Part 2 - With "And is not overcome" - let go of hands, with right arm leading, left hand slightly behind, make graceful turn around right shoulder in six steps on the spot.
Continue.

The Jesus Prayer

11. "The Jesus prayer"

We return to the Jesus Prayer, this time a longer English translation. By "Lord" and "Christ" we express something of our willingness to access help from the One who is greater than ourselves, yet who is readily available in and about us. Words like "mercy" (see 9. "Kyrie") and "sinner" can be uncomfortable for some. "Sinner" is often used simplistically to refer to being or doing "bad". According to its Greek origins, however, it is more about separation from God, "missing the mark", being diverted from the important to the trivial, to forget or be distracted. In this sense "sinning" is when we drift away from what really matters – our search for and relationship to God who is the Way. That is not a call to self denial or sacrifice, rather to discern what is really worthy, to set priorities, to follow what truly has heart and meaning for us and not surrender to the superficial and the transient.

The Dance invites us to take stock, to get grounded in our own bodies, to be open to the spirit of the Divine and embrace it, letting go of the fundamentally meaningless (but often powerful) distractions of everyday reality.

Stand in a circle , hold hands, face centre, spread to make space between and let go of hands. Anticlockwise movement, leading always with right foot.
Part 1 - With "Lord Jesus Christ, Son of God"- hands by side, step right bowing slightly, raise hands and bring together palm over palm and draw inwards to rest over the heart (with quite a firm but gentle, audible slap on the chest). At the same time slide close left foot. Three times.
Part 2 – With "A sinner" - keep hands over heart, bow head and sway right and left. Continue.

When Darkness Falls

A Round

When dark - falls I hear you call: am

I will ne - ver

here, I am here, I am here_____

leave_____

you._____

12. "When darkness falls"

As we deepen our commitment along the Way and our spirituality matures, paradoxically it can often be at this time we feel that even greater, perhaps the greatest, challenges surface for us. The background to this dance lies in a story found in "Coming Home". It can be in our hour of deepest darkness, feeling lost and confused, disconnected from God, that we may find God is present. When we ask "Where are you when I need you?" it may be that the same answer always arises "I am here." We do not just experience God in moments of heavenly bliss, but also in the depths of the abyss (Psalm 139:8). Although there are times when we feel God is absent, there is nowhere that God is not. This song reminds us that when we are at our most lost, that is the time to ask for the One whose help we need, and He will always respond to us in some way. Here it is in words, but it can be in other ways, the sudden feeling of being taken care of, the sense of the Presence, the unexpected offer of help or a hand of friendship. Along the Way we can sometimes feel we are "there" or "on the right track". Then suffering of some sort happens to throw us off centre, disconnect us from God. In this chant we are reminded that no matter how many times we get lost or withdraw or wander, God is always with us forever reminding us of His presence, calling us Home. Sung as a round, this song emphasises the eternal calling of the Divine. The Way is full of times when we will rise and fall, rise and fall...

The Dance reflects that possibility of our standing on holy ground, in the presence of God, even though we may only feel His absence. The response is not one of hopelessness, but one of realisation, of discovery of an eternal truth – that separation from God is only ever an illusion, that ultimately if we allow it (and sometimes if we don't!) God will break through and reach out to us. We stand and move together through the darkness, the footsteps then marking out the star of Bethlehem, the light that shows us the Way in the night. This dance can be enhanced by being candle-lit, with each person holding a candle, letting their own light shine.

Stand in a circle and join hands in "W" position. Adjust hold so that only little fingers are linked. Candles, if used, can be held in the right hand. Clockwise movement, leading always with left foot.
Part 1 - Side left, close right. Four times.
Part 2 - Left foot point forward with toe touching floor in front, then move to side with toe touching again, then point behind, once more with just toe touching. Repeat movement using right foot. During this part of the dance allow your gaze to follow the toes touching the ground – front, side, behind each time.
Continue

Beloved

I am healed by Your love, I am healed by Your love. I be -
My be - lov - ed you are, my be - lov - ed you are; and in

I am healed by Your love, I am healed by Your love. I be -
My be - lov - ed you are, my be - lov - ed you are; and in

long in Your love, I be - long in Your love.
you I am pleased, and in you I am pleased.

long in Your love, I be - long in Your love.
you I am pleased, and in you I am pleased.

13. "Beloved"

In three very different contexts, God expresses his love "for the Beloved" in and with whom He is "pleased" (Matthew 3:17, 12:18 and 17:5) and throughout the Bible we are reminded of the healing power of God's love, most especially in the healing miracles of Jesus. His love for humanity shines through. Along the Way, we discover new depths of Divine love and find that we belong there, that this is our birthright, our natural Home. Consider as you read or sing the words that they are also being spoken directly to each of us (and perhaps back to God); that we are the Beloved Son (or Daughter) in whom the One knows fullness. We are that important in the heart of God, each one of us.

The Dance echoes the profound love between origin and created. Endlessly stepping into the Divine and back again, round and round, connected to each other and to God. Stepping up to God's love, stepping back in wonder at the power of that love and how it heals and connects us all.

Stand in a circle. Join hands basket weave style in front of each other (left hand over top joins right hand underneath of next but one person on right) face centre. Anticlockwise movement. Right step in, close left with gentle bounce, then bounce again on both feet. Side step right close left, once again a gentle bounce as you close and then bounce again with feet together. Step back right close left with a gentle bounce as you do so then bounce once more with feet together. Side step right close left with gentle bounce, then bounce again while feet together. Continue.

Without You

With-out You there is no-thing I can do; oh -

With-out You there is no-thing I can do; oh

With-out You there is no-thing I can do;_____ oh

speak, for Your ser - vant is list - en - ing.

speak, for Your ser - vant is list - en - ing.

speak, for Your ser - vant is list - en - ing_____

14. "Without You"

Along the Way we come to understand our essential powerlessness, or at least the essential powerlessness of the self-centred ego. We come to see ever more deeply that our spiritual quest was really not in our hands (although we might have thought it otherwise at the beginning) and it was the Way which was taking us. In Deuteronomy (32:39) we are reminded of how little control we have (although our egos may tell us otherwise!). So what are we left with? If we are not in charge, who is? In the first book of Samuel (3:7-11) we are given a clear response – "Speak, for your servant is listening". Learning to "listen", to set aside all our own agendas, is a sign of our deepening connection to the Divine. In surrendering our own will, realising our essential powerlessness, we may open to the only source of power which may work through us, its servant not master.

The Dance embodies how we are all in the long chain of existence, in which we learn our true role as servants; followers of the One who went before us. Our spiritual awakening is not concerned with personal pleasure and aggrandisement, but about growing ever closer to God in the long chain of creation and finding our place of service to humanity and all that is.

Stand in a circle, turn to face left. Place your left hand on your heart space and your right hand on the left shoulder of the person in front of you. Clockwise movement. In time to the chant , take a right step forward then left , then right, then rock back (don't move to step back!) onto left foot.
Continue.
(An alternative is for the leader to break free of the circle and guide the group about the room.)

Thy will be done

15. "Thy will be done"

To know deeply our role of service, our spiritual practice involves learning to surrender to (and trust) the Divine will – often the greatest challenge. It can be tough to let go and just trust. But in letting go, we discover a deeper sense of the joy of service, of liberation from the shackles of needing to be in control. If God is in charge, then we can move from a fear based way of being in the world to a place of surrender to the Will, in which we know we are safe, that all will be well, in which we trust.

The Dance has a joyful quality to it, for when we let go of our fear of the loss of ego power, of exercising our own wills, we discover the liberation of what it is to be a servant to a greater Will. We join together and ring the bells of true freedom, raise our palms uppermost in a gesture of our willingness to surrender.

Stand in a circle. No hand hold to start. Anticlockwise movement. Imagine bell chord hanging in front of you.
Part 1 - Rock inward onto right foot, raise hands together in front to grasp bell chord, pull down twice in rhythm to first two "Thy will be done".
Part 2 - Next two "Thy will be done"- let go of bell chord, join hands and step right, then left then let go of hands and make ¾ turn with hands raised to shoulder height palms uppermost. Turn around right shoulder stepping right/left to face centre again.
Continue.

In You (The Waves)

16. "In You (the waves)"

1 Rest in You, rest in You, oh the holy rest in You.
   Rest in You, rest in You, oh the holy rest in You.
   Oh the holy rest in You, rest in You, rest in You.
   Oh the holy rest in You, rest in You, rest in You.

2. Peace in You, peace in You, oh the holy peace in You.
   Peace in You, peace in You, oh the holy peace in You.
   Oh the holy peace in You, peace in You, peace in You.
   Oh the holy peace in You, peace in You, peace in You.

3. Truth in You, truth in You, oh the holy truth in You.
   Truth in You, truth in You, oh the holy truth in You.
   Oh the holy truth in You, truth in You, truth in You.
   Oh the holy truth in You, truth in You, truth in You.

4. Love in You, love in You, oh the holy love in You.
   Love in You, love in You, oh the holy love in You.
   Oh the holy love in You, love in You, love in You.
   Oh the holy love in You, love in You, love in You.

5. Light in You, light in You, oh the holy light in You.
   Light in You, light in You, oh the holy light in You.
   Oh the holy light in You, light in You, light in You.
   Oh the holy light in You, light in You, light in You.

6. Dark in You, dark in You, oh the holy dark in You.
   Dark in You, dark in You, oh the holy dark in You.
   Oh the holy dark in You, dark in You, dark in You.
   Oh the holy dark in You, dark in You, dark in You.

7. Home in You, home in You, oh the holy home in You.
   Home in You, home in You, oh the holy home in You.
   Oh the holy home in You, home in You, home in You.
   Oh the holy home in You, home in You, home in You.

This song emerged whilst walking along a beach on Iona. The waves rushed in, swirled and pulled back, but in diagonals, never returning to quite the same space and always carrying the flotsam and jetsam along with them. The rhythmic, pulsating quality of the waves resonates with our relationship with God, being carried along rather than controlling, ebbing and flowing; a relationship rooted in the myriad qualities of the nature of God (including the darkness of God, not as in evil but as in mystery). God can never be fully comprehended by intellectual processes or theology, but He can be known through experience, feeling – a different level of knowing (faith) beyond words – the "peace" that passes all understanding (Philippians 4:7).

The Dance invites us to embrace the condition of "unknowing" sometimes dancing close to God, sometimes pulling away, but all part of the infinite possibility of relating in the infinite possibility of God.

Stand in a circle, hold hands (V hold). Anticlockwise to start.
Part 1 - Eight grapevine steps to the right (side right, left cross in front, side right, left cross behind, side right left cross in front, side right, left cross behind). Now eight grapevine steps to the left (right cross in front, side left, right cross behind, side left, right cross in front, side left, right cross behind, side left). Part 2 - Four steps diagonally inwards to right of centre, starting with right foot, raising arms high whilst doing so, until at highest at centre. Four steps diagonally backwards to the right, starting with right foot, lower arms to V hold whilst doing so. Repeat this zigzag sequence.
Continue.

All shall be well

17. "All shall be well"

These words are taken from the "shewings" of Mother Julian of Norwich, a great mediaeval mystic who plunged into a boundless relationship with God - and tried to capture her experience in words. This phrase was taken up by Eliot in his wonderful poem "The Four Quartets". It alludes to the experience of deep surrender into the Divine will, through which we let go of our ego agendas of what is good or bad, evil or Divine, but the realisation that somehow, in some way that our limited human consciousness cannot (ever) fully comprehend, God is in control and knows all. Even though we may see a world of duality, of good and evil, of right and wrong, of just and unjust – God knows and is present at an infinitely deeper and incomprehensible way and (reassuringly) beyond limited perceptions and values of time and space. In Him all things are made good. We can relax and let go, and let God be God, not in passivity, but in active service in the world and participating in the Divine will.

The Dance is a prayerful dance of reassurance, a realisation that God is at work in each of us, an encouragement to do what has to be done, to be what we are destined to be, and through which all shall be well. Moving from one to another, we are encouraged, in a world of fear, to know deeply that God is making all things well, way beyond our limited judgements.

Stand in a circle then separate into pairs, face partner.
Part 1 - Place right hand over heart centre, left hand over right hand of partner. Look into each other's eyes while singing the first two sequences of "And all shall be well and all shall be well" then slowly let go of partner and move your hands into prayer position whilst slowly making low bow to partner and singing second part of chant "All manner of thing shall be well".
Part 2 Either move in sequence to the next person facing you in the circle, or move at random around the room for next partner.
Continue.

Gloria

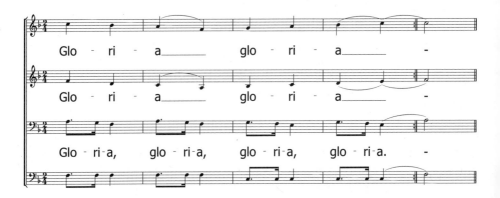

18. "Gloria"

As we draw ever closer to Home along the Way, as the soul comes nearer to the One from which it came, after (what seems like) a long journey a celebratory quality emerges. Not only celebratory (rightly so) at finding our hearts' desire but also awestruck by the nature of the Divine whose nature is beyond our full comprehension, yet closer and more intimate than our own breath. There are many biblical references to the glory of God – that compelling, radiant, awesome, infinite, unconquerable nature of God's love. The whole creation sings of this glory (Psalm 19:1, Isaiah 6:3, Luke 2:14, John 1:14 for example). In the poem "Beloved" (due for publication in summer 2010) I note how, "When I come, I come in glory, and there is no power on earth can stand against me." Aware of that glory, there is nothing left to do but bathe in it, shout its name, receive it.

The Dance is essentially celebratory and worshipful. We move in harmony with each other, the light of each of us merged with the light of the Divine, a grand vista of union, a place of absolute connection with the One, so that there may indeed be no sense of separation at all.

Stand in a circle and into partners. This dance needs at least 16 people in pairs otherwise the circles are too cramped. If the group is too small, or you prefer not to have a partner dance, it can be done using one circle only.
If dancing with partners, tallest partner stands behind smallest to form outer and inner circle! Partner at outer circle takes small step to right to position behind the space of the two people in front. The steps throughout have a smooth and gliding quality rather than bouncing or skipping.
Part 1 - Both inner and outer circle start with right foot. Each circle joins hands - V hold. Outer circle eight steps to right at same time as inner circle eight steps to left. The outer circle eight steps to left at same time as inner circle eight steps to right. Thus returning to original position.
Part 2 - Starting with right foot, everybody takes four steps inwards with hands in W hold. Then everybody steps backwards starting with right foot, four steps with hands lowering to V hold. All step inwards again four steps, with outer circle taking arms over heads of inner circle. All step backwards four steps (start with right foot) as the two circles become one now in a basket weave hold. (if you are not using the partner dance, these last two stages are modified, simply stepping in and out with the same number of steps but not "capturing" – as one circle.)
Part 3 - Anticlockwise – all side right close left eight times.
Part 4 - All step inward starting with right foot, then four steps outwards starting with right foot. Then starting with right foot go inward 2nd time four steps, outer circle lift arms while doing so, over head of inner circle and release inner circle. Both circles then step outwards four steps again, beginning with right foot. Thus returning to two separate circles. (Again, this last part is modified if there is only one circle).
Continue.

I love you

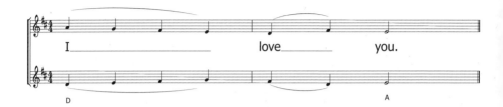

I _____ love _____ you.

D   A

19. "I love You"

We have come full circle or perhaps completed a path around a spiral, coming to know our
relationship with the Divine and yet not quite returning to the same place. God is infinite
and the soul is of God, so the soul is infinite too. There are no limits to our exploration of our
relationship with, in and to God. But above and beyond all is a deep knowing of the love of
God for us personally that we explored in Isaiah 43 (dance 3); coming to rest in this knowing
we are able to let go of obstructions in ourselves. Healed by the love of God, we can love God
completely as He loves us; and more, to love our neighbour as ourselves (Mark 12:31). We
sing "I love You" to God, to all that is, and open to God singing the same words to us.

The Dance is a repetition of the first, but with a subtle difference. We no longer stand alone.
As Eliot (in the Four Quartets) reminds us, we have arrived where we started but know the
place for the first time. The journey was not to somewhere or someone other, but to ourselves,
to know love, to know God more deeply. Our hearts can be more open. We no longer stand
alone, for we realise all human beings seek and inherently know the same love that binds all
the creation together.

*Stand close together in a circle, join hands (V hold), legs slightly apart, with upper arms
touching neighbour. Sway gently to the rhythm of the chant from side to side (four beats each
way). All swaying together, start by swaying together to right. Eyes closed.
Continue.*

Notes:

Notes: